the very best

food and drink

websites

Zingin.com

Prentice
Hall

An Imprint of Pearson Education

London New York Toronto Sydney Tokyo
Singapore Madrid Mexico City Munich Paris

PEARSON EDUCATION LIMITED

Head Office:
Edinburgh Gate
Harlow
Essex CM20 2JE
Tel: +44 (0)1279 623623
Fax: +44 (0)1279 431059

London Office:
128 Long Acre
London WC2E 9AN
Tel: +44 (0)20 7447 2000
Fax: +44 (0)20 7240 5771

First published in Great Britain in 2000

ISBN 0-130-32984-3

The right of Paul Carr to be identified as author of
this work has been asserted by it in accordance with the
Copyright, Designs and Patents Act 1988.

British Library Cataloguing-in-Publication Data
A catalogue record for this book can be obtained from the British Library.

Many of the designations used by manufacturers and sellers to
distinguish their products are claimed as trademarks. Pearson Education
Limited has made every attempt to supply trademark information about
manufacturers and their products mentioned in this book.

10 9 8 7 6 5 4 3 2 1

Typeset by Land & Unwin (Data Sciences) Ltd
Printed and bound by Ashford Colour Press, Gosport, Hampshire

The publisher's policy is to use paper manufactured from sustainable forests.

contents

introduction

A quick snack on the move... a meal for the kids... a cocktail after work... fast food... or a full gourmet feast. Whatever you're hungry for – the internet makes it easy to arrange.

Ever since someone people started to realise that the web was a great way to swap recipes and culinary tips, the amount of food and drink related material online has continued to grow. Today, you can choose between millions of pages of information on everything from planning a dinner party to finding your nearest real ale pub. The difficult part is knowing which ones are worthy of your attention and which are just a waste of web space.

When we originally launched Zingin.com the plan was to create a user-friendly, UK-focused guide to the best of the web. Although the site itself has grown rapidly since those early days, we're still very choosy about which sites we recommend to our users.

With this in mind, when we decided to put this book together we were determined not to create just another huge list of food and drink sites – there's enough of them around and they just add to the confusion. Instead, we've tried to provide a user-friendly guide to the best of the culinary web. From cocktail recipes to restaurant reviews, diet advice to doughnuts and everything in between – if it's useful and relevant, you'll find it here – if it's not, you won't.

So who is the book written for? Well, if you're a UK user

who wants to get straight to the best internet food and drink resources then it's for you! Wine buffs, restaurateurs, amateur chefs, parents, students – even food critics – no matter what your interest in food, we'll help you find what you're looking for.

We've tried to make it as easy as possible for you just to dive in and get started with the book. The chapters have been put in a (hopefully) logical order, starting with general food sites, then those that offer huge numbers of tempting recipes, followed by more specific food and drink resources and finally, if you don't fancy spending time in the kitchen, a run down of the best restaurants and take-away outlets.

Although only the very best of the web has made it into these pages, we've headed up each section with **the best of the best** so you don't have to waste any time getting started, and if you know the name of the site you want, you can look it up in the quick reference section tucked away neatly at the back.

With the help of this book it should be pretty straight-forward to find the information you're looking for but if you do have any problems please come and visit us on the web (**www.zingin.com**) and we'll try our best to help you out.

Bon Appetit!

Paul Carr
Founder
Zingin.com

the internet:
a (very) brief guide

The fact that you've bought this book means that you've probably used the internet before, either at home or at work. If, however, you're still getting to grips with the basics then read on for the answers to some of our most frequently asked questions.

Getting started

There are plenty of online resources to help you get the most out of the web but none of them are any use if you're not online. By far the quickest way to get started is to pop into your local newsagent or computer shop and get hold of one of the zillions of free internet access CDs stuck to the front of popular computer magazines. However, if you want a bit more information before taking the plunge have a quick look at the following pointers.

I'm new to the internet, how do I get started?

It goes without saying that to take advantage of the information contained in this book, you'll need access to the internet. If you want to connect from home you'll need a computer (a 486 or above should be fine), a modem (new computers usually come with one built in) and a spare telephone socket within easy reach of the computer.

The modem, which plugs in to the back of your computer (unless it's already built in) and then into the telephone socket, has basically one purpose – to allow your computer to send and receive data over a telephone line. Once you're plugged in, all that remains now is to decide which internet service provider (ISP) you will use to connect to the 'net. Your ISP provides a gateway to the internet and when you ask your computer to connect to the web or to send and receive e-mails, your modem is actually dialling into their network which, in turn, is connected to the rest of the internet. This explains how you can send an e-mail to Egypt or to Edinburgh for the same price – you're only paying for the call to the ISP (the price of a local call or less). If you don't want to connect from home then most large libraries provide free or low-cost internet access and there are plenty of internet cafés around the country who will be happy to help you take your first online steps.

Which ISP is right for me?

Choosing an ISP can be a complicated business with some companies offering free access, some offering free telephone calls and a few still clinging on to monthly charges – all trying to persuade you that you'll get a better deal with them. Pretty confusing. Basically, the right ISP for you will depend on what you want to use the internet for.

If you're only interested in e-mail, surfing the web and maybe building a personal website then you'll be fine with a free service. Of course, there's no such thing as a free lunch and you'll usually still have to pay either local call charges or a fixed fee for unlimited access. Luckily for internet users, there's fierce competition between ISPs and you can find some excellent deals if you shop around. To get online with a free service you can either pick up a connection CD from one of the high street shops who have set up their own ISPs (WHSmiths, PC World, Waterstones and Tesco to name just a few) or call up one of the providers advertised in any of the popular internet magazines.

If you want to use the internet for business and require extra features such as high speed access, a business website or your own domain name (e.g. **you@yourname.com**) then you'll need use a specialist ISP who will usually charge a monthly fee in addition to your normal phone charges.

If you already have internet access at work, university, school or in a local internet café then surf over to ISP Review (**www. ispreview.co.uk**) for a full run-down of the best and worst UK internet service providers.

Online help and advice

Ok, so you've made it online and you're looking for help and advice on how to get the most out of the web? Of course, to find the best websites to get you started you'll want to take a quick trip to your friends at Zingin.com (**www.zingin.com**) but for technical support and general advice, try these.

Why does it say that the page I'm looking for is not found?

The internet is in a constant state of development and things are getting moved around and deleted all the time. Anyone who's spent more than a couple of minutes on the web will have clicked on a link or typed in a web address only to get hit with the dreaded 'File not found' message. If the page you're looking for seems to have vanished, the most likely cause is that the page has been deleted or moved to another address. If an address doesn't work, try removing bits from the end until you find something. For example, if the address **www.asite.com/directory/files/filename.html** produces an error, try deleting the 'filename.html' bit to see if there's anything at **www.asite.com/directory/files**. If you're still getting an error then try **www.asite.com/directory** and finally **www.asite.com**. If you run out of things to delete and still can't find the site then it's probably temporarily unavailable or has been deleted. Sites that have been moved can often be tracked down using a search engine such as Google (**www.google.com**) – simply type in the name of the page/site and see what comes up.

What is the best software for browsing the web?

Most of the free ISPs include a copy of Microsoft Internet Explorer on their access disks and, unless you really want to, there's no real need to use another browser. If you do fancy a change or want to fight back against Microsoft's quest for world domination, there are some alternatives worth trying. The best of the bunch is Netscape Navigator which contains a very similar range of features to Internet Explorer but with slightly less polish. The best way to describe Netscape is like Burger King to Microsoft's McDonald's – try them both and decide which one tastes better. Other choices can be found at **www.browserwatch.com**.

How can I find out more about using the web?

The internet used to be controlled by academics, scientists and computer geeks and unless you knew your way around it could be very scary indeed. In cyberspace no one could hear you scream.

Nowadays, using e-mail and surfing the web is like driving a car – pretty straightforward when you get the hang of it even if you don't know exactly what's going on under the bonnet. Having said that, if you want to get the most out of your internet experience you'll need to get a basic grasp of the way it works. One of the best guides to how the 'net works and what it can do is Learn the Net (**www.learnthenet.com**) which contains some very well-written tutorials covering e-mail, downloading files, building a website and plenty of other useful stuff. If you're baffled by internet jargon you'll definitely want to have a quick look at PC Webopedia (**www.pcwebopedia.com**) and for beginner's advice with a UK perspective surf over to BBC Webwise (**www.bbc.co.uk/webwise**).

Buying online

Throughout this book you'll find sites that allow you to order products, book tickets and generally spend your hard-earned cash. The first thing to remember is that using your credit card online is 100% safe providing you take a few sensible precautions.

How do I know which companies to trust?

Firstly, wherever possible stick to companies you've heard of. If someone you know has bought from a particular site without any problems or if it's a household name then the risk is greatly reduced.

As with any purchase on or off the web, you should always ensure that you are buying from a reputable company. Sites such as Amazon (**www.amazon.co.uk**) and Last Minute (**www.lastminute.com**) are very well-known internet traders and so are a risk-free option but if you do want to order from a company you've never heard of then take a look at the next few questions which will hopefully address your concerns.

Can hackers get hold of my credit card number once I've typed it in?

As long as you only type your credit card details into sites that offer encryption security (SSL), your information will be perfectly safe. Look for a yellow padlock on the bottom right of your browser window if you are using Internet Explorer or, in Netscape, look for a closed padlock. This ensures that information sent to the site is encrypted and so cannot be intercepted by hackers. If the site is not secure, be very wary about placing an online order and *never* send credit card information via normal e-mail.

How can I check on the status of my order?

Many larger sites offer order tracking facilities which allow you to check the progress of your order until it is delivered. If there is no order tracking, ensure there is a contact telephone number in case you need to chase things up.

Is it safe to order from outside the UK?

Orders placed with companies outside the UK are not protected by UK sale of goods or safety legislation. Only order from abroad if you know and trust the company you are dealing with and even then, try to stick within Western Europe and the USA.

Am I going to get stung by hidden costs?

There's no 'internet tax' for orders made online but as with any mail order purchase you should always check whether your order includes postage and packing costs. Also, remember that orders from outside the UK may be subject to additional customs and import costs.

Is there a regulatory body for online traders?

The Consumers Association have been looking after the interests of shoppers for years and have recently launched a scheme to protect you on the web. The Which? Webtrader scheme (**www.which.net/webtrader**) requires its members to abide by a strict code of conduct if they want to join. Sites that have the Webtrader logo have to provide a decent level of service otherwise Which? will simply kick them out! It's worth remembering that membership of the scheme isn't compulsory and many reputable businesses are not members, so if you don't see the logo don't assume the worst, but if you do – expect the best.

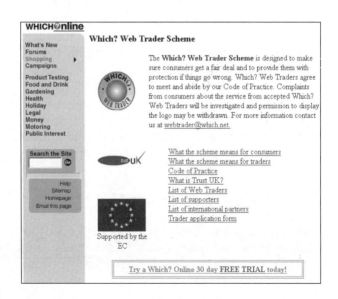

What if the goods don't arrive or my credit card is used fraudulently?

Don't panic if products ordered online take a while to arrive. Just like in the real world, delays do happen and things can be out of stock – even if you receive a confirmation saying that everything is fine. However, if you've waited longer than 21 days then you should contact the company concerned to hurry them up.

A gentle reminder will usually be enough to get things moving but if you're still not getting anywhere you should contact your credit card issuer for advice. If the site is a member of the Which? Webtrader scheme, make sure you let them know as well.

If you have problems with an order made using a credit card, you will usually be able to recover any lost money from your card issuer. If you're concerned about fraud, call your credit card company to check their policy regarding fraudulent transactions.

Can I buy anything I like over the web?

Yes and no. Yes, most things are available – from sweets and cakes to cars and houses but, no, you can't necessarily order them from the UK. The law on ordering from abroad using the internet is the same as using the phone and there are certain products which it is illegal to bring into the country. Some good examples of this are: drugs, certain food items, adult material, pets and automatic weapons. You can probably guess the law's position on drugs and guns but if you need to check out what is allowed, visit Customs and Excise (www.hmce.gov.uk).

For the full low-down on internet shopping, check out the Zingin's *The very best shopping websites*.

Searching the web

Finding what you're looking for on the internet can be like trying to find a very small needle in a very large haystack. Search engines are fine if you're looking for very specialist information (the population of Peru or the Belgian translation of *Romeo and Juliet*) but when it comes to popular subjects like travel or music it's easy to get swamped by the number of sites available.

So how do you find the information you need without wading through pages of irrelevant junk? Good question...

What is the best search engine?

That all depends on what you're looking for. There are literally thousands of search engines and directory sites and each has its own strengths and weaknesses.

For general searches we recommend Google (www.google.com) which ranks sites on both relevance and popularity (how many other sites link to them). You'll usually find the information you want on the first page of results but if you have no success, try the same search on Hotbot (www.hotbot.com) and Altavista (www.altavista.co.uk).

If you are looking for UK-specific information there are plenty of home-grown search engines which should fit the bill. A couple of our favourites are UK Plus (www.ukplus.co.uk) and Search UK (www.searchuk.co.uk).

How do I find a business or service?

Looking for a plumber? An electrician? A four-star hotel in Derby? Rather than reaching for the *Yellow Pages*, take a wander over to Scoot (**www.scoot.co.uk**) which will let you search by business type, location or the name of the company you need. If you prefer to use good old *Yellow Pages* then it can be found at Yell (**www.yell.com**).

Is it really possible to get free software over the internet? Where can I find it?

The internet is full of free software, much of which can be downloaded for just the price of a telephone call. Generally, unless you are willing to spend some money, you will only be able to get a trial version of the program which will stop working after a short period of time (usually 30 days). If you want to carry on using it after that you'll have to pay for it – often at a substantial discount over the normal retail price. To get your hands on the best of the freebies, try searching Download.com (www.download.com) and Tucows (www.tucows.com).

Where can I find the best online shops?

As the number of internet traders has increased, so have the directories that promise to tell you where to find them. One of the most popular shopping directories is Shopsmart (www.shopsmart.com) but our personal favourite is 2020 Shops (www.2020shops.com) which provides friendly reviews of each of the stores and a useful rating system to help you get started. If you want to compare prices before you buy, you can shop around quickly and easily with the excellent Hoojit (www.hoojit.com) or Kelkoo (uk.kelkoo.com).

So many search engines, so little time – is there an alternative?

Funny you should ask! You can access the search engines listed above directly from The Zingin Search Guide (www.zingin.com/ guide/search) and there's a complete listing of UK and global search tools in our Information Guide (www.zingin.com/guide/ info/search).

food and drink portals

The web is a great source of food and drink information and is packed full with all the information you need to prepare a meal, a snack, a feast or a banquet. However, before you start dredging the web for culinary content, check out one of the popular food portals which offer a virtual smorgasbord of recipes, ingredients, healthy eating ideas, menu planners and a simple way of finding other relevant sites and resources.

General portals

Rather than focusing on a particular type of food, the web's general food and drink portals cover the complete spectrum of food types, no matter whether you're a beginner or a connoisseur. For dedicated recipe resources see Recipe databases in Chapter 3.

■ The best of the best

Simply Food **www.simplyfood.co.uk**
Carlton have developed some truly top-class websites both to promote their existing brands and also to develop new

ones. Simply Food falls into both categories – a Carlton production in its own right which also just happens to promote the Carlton Food Network (CFN) from time to time. A recipe finder, wine guides, news, reviews, features and even a section dedicated to the joys of chocolate provide something for everyone and the CFN tie-in means that there are plenty of celebrity chefs on hand to provide additional advice. If you don't fancy cooking, you'll also find plenty of restaurant information, food events and profiles of the world's top chefs – and you can buy all of your recipe books and kitchen gadgets in the secure online store.

■ *The rest of the best*

Epicurious food.epicurious.com

A close contender for the top spot, the only thing that counted against Epicurious is the fact that it's so obviously aimed at an American audience. Having said that, if you don't mind not being able to take full advantage of the well-stocked online shop, you will love the site which claims to be 'for people who eat'. The usual mix of menus, advice and features are all present and correct but it's the other features that make the site such a joy to use; forums and chat rooms to swap ideas with your fellow gastronomes, mouth-watering food photography and the superb recipe file – a searchable database of over 11,000 recipes. All in all, if you love food – you'll adore Epicurious.

Food 'n' Drink www.foodndrink.co.uk

Not only does Food 'n' Drink laugh in the face of the word 'and', it's also one of the funkiest food sites on the web. Beyond the bright orange, split-screen front page, you'll find news, reviews, gossip, restaurant guides and, er, pretty much everything you'll find on the other food sites. The difference here is in the presentation which may not be the slickest in the world but somehow manages to make the site feel warm, welcoming and personal – and you can even join the Food 'n' Drink club which will save you money in some of the UK's top eateries. Attractive 'n' functional.

Out of the Frying Pan www.outofthefryingpan.com

If you thought Food 'n' Drink was trying hard to be cool, just wait 'til you see this supremely 'in ya face' food portal. Out of the Frying Pan is part of the Chick Click network, a group of American sites which target the strong and sassy surfer, and if you've encountered any of their other sites you'll know what to expect. Well-written articles with an emphasis on fun, competitions, recipes, profiles of leading female chefs ('queens of cuisine'), kitchen gadgets and so much more make this an essential bookmark for foody females (and brave men). Think Delia Smith meets the Spice Girls.

Handbag Food www.handbag.com/food

Handbag, one of the UK's leading women's portals, have done well with their extremely impressive Food channel. You'll find the usual stuff plus a useful question and answer feature, shopping and more than a smattering of celebrities – Gordon Ramsey being the celeb de jour when we surfed in. Well done.

BBC Food and Drink www.bbc.co.uk/foodanddrink

If celebrity chefs are your cup of tea then you'll be spoilt for choice on the official site of the BBC's *Food and Drink* programme. Jilly Goolden and Oz Clarke aside, there's plenty of menu advice, cunningly separated into starters, meat, fish, vegetarian, side dishes and desserts – and a nifty recipe finder to help you plan your next meal. There may not be the same depth here as you'll find on the likes of Epicurious and Simply Food but, for fans of the programme, it can't be beaten.

Foodlines www.foodlines.com

Do you have a passion for food? If so, this site has been designed for you. As with most of the food portals, the key-stone here is the recipe archive, which is separated into an impressive number of easy-to-browse categories, making it extremely simple to find something suitable from a light snack to a full gourmet feast. To complement the recipes, you'll also find healthy eating advice, an events listing, news, features and a wealth of resources for food lovers around the world.

E Food www.e-food.com

Another American food site, with noticeably less content than the *big two* but still offering plenty for food lovers to get their teeth into. Admittedly, unless you're planning a visit to the US or Argentina, you'll have to ignore the restaurant listings and takeaway menus but the food news and articles are first rate – one of them, when we last visited, having been sourced from that well-respected food publication *The News of the World* (it's true!). Not brilliant but well worth a look.

About Home Cooking homecooking.about.com

We can always rely on our chums at About to provide a decent site, regardless of subject – and this one is no different. About's guide to Home Cooking features links, forums, recipes (surprise!) and is a great way to track down the best food resources the web has to offer.

CD Kitchen www.cdkitchen.com

Like so many other sites in this category, CD Kitchen claims to be your complete cooking resource and, like so many other sites, it is thoroughly deserving of the title. Over 4500 recipes, including some copies of famous brands (Kentucky Fried Chicken, Burger King Fries etc.) plus a wealth of cooking tips, hints and links to the rest of the culinary web.

Kitchen Link **www.kitchenlink.com**

Looking for something that's not covered here? Kitchen link provides links to more than 10,000 food and drink sites on the web. Check out Chef Heaven (**www.chefheaven.com**) for more of the same.

■ *The best of the rest*

Global Gourmet **www.globalgourmet.com**

Incorporating Foodwine.com and the Electronic Gourmet Guide, this impressive American site concentrates on well-written and entertaining features rather than design.

Food.com **www.food.com**

Despite the fact that half the site is interesting only to American users – unless you're wondering where you can get a takeaway in Florida – this well-presented site still has plenty for international visitors. Worth a look.

Food Forum **www.foodforum.org**

Partially funded by the European Commission, The Food Forum is both a place for chefs to discuss their trade and for aspiring chefs to become inspired. Looks great. For more industry-type news check out The Internet Food Channel (**www.foodchannel.com**).

Internet Chef **www.ichef.com**

Tens of thousands of recipes, tricks, tips and a whole world of links to the best foody stuff on the web.

Wine and Dine **www.winedine.co.uk**

No-frills electronic magazine for lovers of wine, restaurants and travel. The design is uninspiring but the content, if you like the writing style, is superb.

Specialist portals

Fancy a Chinese? Curry? Irish? Whatever your taste in food, there's bound to be a specialist portal all about it. Recipes, restaurant reviews and features are usually the order of the day (no pun intended) but look out for chat forums and even online ingredients shopping.

■ The best of the best

Chopstix www.chopstix.co.uk
A dedicated Chinese food portal, packed full of expert features, a daily recipe, and a veritable wok full of oriental goodness. Whether you just enjoy a chow mein or you're a professional chef, you'll find something for you – and by using the expert guide to Chinese cooking and ingredients, you can progress from the former to the latter in next to no time.

■ The rest of the best

Sanjeev Kapoor www.sanjeevkapoor.com
Ok, it's confession time – we had no idea who Sanjeev Kapoor was until we discovered his excellent site. Apparently 'Master chef Sanjeev Kapoor is best known for his TV show Khana Khazana, a weekly program on Zee TV' – so now you know. Confirming his celebrity status as the Gary Rhodes of Indian cuisine, Mr Kapoor has developed a suitably profes-

sional site which not only showcases his own creations but also allows visitors to post their own. As well as the recipes, there's also a comprehensive guide to everything else you could possibly want to know, including preparation, storage, nutrition and even a slightly bizarre 3D microwave. Hot.

Dr Gourmet www.drgourmet.com

If healthy eating is your thing, you'll be in de-toxifying heaven here. Dr Gourmet is, in fact, Dr Timothy Harlan who seems to be something of a health evangelist. Despite the off-puttingly healthy-sounding recipes, the food actually does look very nice, proving that there is a tasty alternative to pizza and chips.

Irish Food www.irishfood.com

The name says it all really. Recipes, Irish restaurant reviews and links to ingredient suppliers and Irish cook books make this a thoroughly enjoyable guide to emerald eating. Dig deeply though, there's much more to the site than you'd think from the front page.

Veg Web www.vegweb.com

The cluttered design of Veg Web should come with a health warning as it's likely to seriously damage your ability to navigate. The links are all over the place and there seems to be no sign of a coherent menu system but if you enjoy a challenge, there's plenty of excellent content to be found, including a culinary dictionary, recipe exchange, e-mail newsletter and even vegetarian poetry (what rhymes with potato?). There are certainly more slick veggie sites on the web but few of them match Veg Web's depth of content.

3

recipes and ingredients

It's time to cut to the chase. Forget food news, restaurant reviews and 3D utensils – where's the best place to find recipes? As luck would have it, the web is packed full of recipe sites containing literally hundreds of thousands of dishes covering the entire culinary spectrum, from traditional English fare to proper Japanese Sushi – and if you're looking for information about a particular ingredient, you'll find it here in spades. In short, whatever you're making – the internet makes it easier.

Recipe databases

Food, glorious food, at the click of a mouse is the name of the game here. Browse by style and ingredients, search for your favourite dish or sign up for an e-mail recipe a day, it's all possible and it's all free. If you're looking for inspiration, your first stop should be one of the huge recipe database sites which offer thousands of choices, while, for more specific tastes, you'll find a wealth of specialist recipe listings to help you out.

■ *The best of the best*

All Recipes www.allrecipes.com

You'll never suffer from chef's block again once you've visited this excellent site which contains more recipes than we ever thought existed. All Recipes actually consists of a number of specialist sites, focusing on different types of foods, including **chickenrecipe.com**, **barbequerecipe.com**, **pastarecipe.com** and even the calorie-filled **pierecipe.com** – you can browse each site separately or search the whole lot by keyword. The recipes themselves are predictably excellent with clear instructions so that even the most hardened cookerphobe can get stuck in, and the site looks great and is a breeze to navigate. Now, if only there was a kebabrecipe.com, life would be perfect.

■ *The rest of the best*

Recipe Center **www.recipecenter.com**

Not quite as polished as All Recipes but impressive none-theless, Recipe Center (note the American spelling) claims to contain over 100,000 recipes and, by allowing visitors to add their own favourites, that figure is set to increase. Even if you're not planning on doing any cooking, you'll find plenty to whet your appetite (anyone had enough of the food puns yet?) with some excellent food photography, recipe forums and even a fact of the day – 'did you know that a tomato is actually a fruit?'. Well... yes, actually.

Recipe a Day **www.recipe-a-day.com**

Go on, have a wild stab in the dark, guess at what's on offer here. Yup, that's right – simply sign up using your e-mail address and they'll send you a new recipe every single day of the week. Just in case one recipe isn't enough to satisfy your hunger for inspiration, you can browse through the archive of previous editions, which is also useful for finding out what to expect before signing up. Splendid.

Betty Crocker **www.bettycrocker.com**

America's answer to Mrs Beaton is one of the USA's most famous celebrity chefs. Her articles are published in hun-dreds of newspapers, she's a TV regular and her recipes are a benchmark for culinary quality. Now Betty's hit the web with this well-designed site with lots of recipes, practical advice and tips for reluctant cooks. It's glossy, it's *very* American and we love it.

Veggie Heaven www.veggieheaven.com

Created and maintained by Rosamond Richardson, one of the UK's most innovative vegetarian cookery writers (according to the site's introductory blurb), Veggie Heaven is certainly a divine source of meat-free meals and features. Over 230 recipes are featured, with easy-to-follow instructions and handy tips to keep you on the right track – and, if you prefer a less digital format, you can even buy Rosamond's paperback recipe book.

My Meals www.my-meals.com

Food sites seem to be obsessed with numbers. All of them boast how many recipes they contain – without any regard to the adage of quality over quantity. My Meals claims a respectable 10,000 dishes and, with their powerful search tool, it's easy enough to find the one you're after. The focus here seems to be on meals that are quick and easy to prepare rather than those that use complicated ingredients and take hours to put together. Ideal when you're cooking in a hurry.

Tu Docs www.tudocs.com

TU ('The Ultimate') Docs is a recipe site – plain and simple. No flashy design, no colour photographs or big prize competitions, just a great range of food to suit all tastes and budgets, all graded for quality and taste.

■ The best of the rest

Good Cooking www.goodcooking.com

A useful no-frills cooking resource, featuring the usual range of recipes and features in an easy-to-browse format. Well worth a look.

Meals for You **www.mealsforyou.com**

Huge food database site, making it easy to track down that elusive favourite recipe.

Alternative recipes

Bored with cottage pie and beans on toast? If you fancy something a little different, why not try some of our favourite alternative recipe sites for inspiration?

■ *The best of the best*

Top Secret Recipes **www.topsecretrecipes.com**

From McDonald's sweet and sour sauce to KFC's coleslaw, now you can re-create your favourite big-brand foods from the comfort of your own kitchen. The site is based in the

good 'ol US of A so don't be surprised if you've not heard of some of the recipes – but they're all worth trying and most of them taste great – trust us, we've tried them. For more of the same, try Copy Kat (**www.copykat.com**).

■ The rest of the best

Eat Bugs **www.eatbugs.com**

Subtitled 'more than you ever wanted to know about eating bugs', this is certainly not one for the fussy eater. If, on the other hand, you fancy a quick meal (worm) or you want to impress the opposite sex with your culinary courage then the recipes actually sound quite tempting. Having said that, with phrases like 'add ant larvae to taste', you're on your own with this one. Still got a craving for creepy crawlies? Try Nature Node (**www.naturenode.com/recipes/recipes_insects.html**).

Sticky Rice **www.stickyrice.com**

It may be nowhere near as daunting as eating bugs but munching on raw fish is not everyone's cup of saki. If you're yet to try Sushi or you would like to know more about preparing it, the amusingly titled Sticky Rice site is a great place to start – with its selection of recipes, advice and everything else you need to start enjoying this surprisingly delicious delicacy.

Ingredients

Hundreds of billions of recipes are no use at all without the right ingredients – and having a cupboard full of ingredients is a bit pointless if you don't know where and how to use them. As luck would have it, there are plenty of sites focusing on specific foods and extras. From pasta to pumpkins, spice to sardines – you'll find more than you could ever need to know about your favourite gastronomic building blocks. If you want to buy ingredients over the web, check out Chapter 9 Shopping.

◼ *The best of the best*

I Love Pasta **www.ilovepasta.org**

Suitably gushing site from America's National Pasta Association (NPA), extolling the virtues of everyone's favourite Italian export. Over 250 NPA-approved recipes,

pasta photography, diet and nutrition advice and plenty of twists, shells and ravioli make this a thoroughly enjoyable site – especially for starving students and vegetarians (or starving vegetarian students).

■ The rest of the best

Spice Guide www.spiceguide.com

Offering a wealth of spice advice – their words, not ours – this site from Tone Brothers, one of America's leading spice companies, offers recipes, a spice encyclopaedia, a kids' corner and even a gripping history of spice. Pah, and you thought spice was boring!

Cheese.com www.cheese.com

So many possible puns, so little time. The imaginatively titled Cheese.com lists over 500 different varieties, complete with information about taste, country of origin and even texture, allowing you to explore the entire smelly spectrum without having to visit a French hypermarket. Fromage fans rejoice!

■ The best of the rest

Jersey Royals www.jerseyroyals.co.uk

It's a site about potatoes. That's all you need to know.

Nutrasweet www.nutrasweet.co.uk

Is Nutrasweet an ingredient? No matter, you can find out all about the calorie-free additive on this fun-packed site. More of the same at Sweet 'n' Low (www.sweetnlow.co.uk) or, for a less tooth-friendly option, check out Tate and Lyle (www.tate-lyle.co.uk).

Pillsbury www.pillsbury.com

America's favourite pastry producer hits the web with this quite impressive site. Must have cost them a fair bit of dough. Ha ha.

Uncle Bens www.unclebens.com

Stirring site from the time-saving sauce and rice people. Product info and pictures aplenty.

Popular food brands

Although not, strictly speaking, ingredients, the following popular food brands form an essential part of the British diet. Unlike the other sections, it's impossible to choose a the best of the best brand site, as it all depends on your taste – from Ben & Jerry's (www.benjerry.co.uk) to Wrigley's, we love 'em all. For shops' own brands (Tesco etc.) and specialist retailers (Thorntons et al.), see Chapter 9 Shopping.

Ben & Jerry's www.benjerry.co.uk

You'd expect something a little off-beat from the creators of Chunky Monkey and Phish Food – and this bright and colourful official site doesn't fail to impress. Plenty of family-friendly info, the usual product blurb and even a bit of history thrown in for good measure. Phabulous. For a more refined choice, try Haagen Dazs (www.haagen-dazs.com).

Bendicks of Mayfair www.bendicks.co.uk

Sophisticated chocolate heaven from one of London's most established and respected confectioners. As is so often the

case with established, expensive brands, the site's design feels a little dated but with a monthly challenge and the latest product information, the content itself is bang up to date.

Birds Eye www.birdseye.com

The first thing you notice, or rather don't notice, when you arrive at the frozen food giant's official site is the absence of Captain Birdseye. Ok, so he's a bit past it now, despite his recent younger reincarnation, but it would still have been nice to see the old guy. Cultural icons aside, there's still plenty to see, including serving suggestions, special offers, product information and even some animated broccoli which welcomes you to the children's fun stuff section. Nice, but it would be better with the Captain.

Cadbury's www.cadbury.co.uk

Everyone loves Cadbury's chocolate! Well, we do anyway – which is why we loved this glass and a half of online goodness. The main Cadbury site is pretty impressive in itself, with a history of chocolate, a chocolate encyclopaedia and even some chocolaty downloads, but it's also well worth checking out the links to the official sites for the likes of Dairy Milk, Cadbury Land and Yowie, each with their own range of downloads, features and games. A deceptively large web presence, spread over a number of sites which should prove popular with both kids and adults.

Campbell Soup www.campbellsoup.com

Another impressive-looking American corporate site, this time for the soup made famous for more than five minutes by Andy Warhol. No sign of pop art here, though, with the emphasis strongly on creating a community of soup lovers – and we're not talking tramps here. The predictable array of serving suggestions and recipes are here and if the sickly sweet imagery of the site is too much for you, you'll be please to hear that meal ideas can be sent to you via e-mail. Nice but cute.

Fisherman's Friend www.fishermansfriend.co.uk

They may be a humble lozenge but Fisherman's Friend have an interesting history – at least that's what this flashy site would have you believe. Everything you never wanted to know about FF, a guide to varieties around the world – Apple and Cinnamon, anyone? – and plenty of cool animated bits make this an entertaining way to waste five minutes.

Fyffe's www.fyffes.com

Considering the size of Fyffe's business we'd expect something more impressive from this site. Separated into 'fun' and 'business' sections, the former contains games, recipes, the banana story and a cheeky animated banana while the latter deals with the less exciting business of actually selling fruit.

Heinz www.heinz.co.uk

Heinz's main site is a pretty formal affair with product info, business information and news, but thrill seekers will be pleased to find links to a surprisingly hip salad crème shrine and the superb Heinz Direct (www.heinz-direct.co.uk) which allows you to order your favourite products for delivery straight to your door – see Chapter 9 Shopping for more details. Look out for the gallery of classic Heinz advertising.

Haribo www.haribo.com

Haribo macht kinder froh und erwachsene ebenso – apparently. Yes, this is a multilingual site but Haribo have kindly provided an English version for UK visitors. Despite being aimed at kids, the site has avoided the temptation to fill every inch of space with cartoon pictures and pictures of products. The products and characters *are* here, but only in moderation and everything is easy enough to navigate – also, if you're feeling mean, you can let your kids browse the German language version and watch their confused little faces. Or not.

Hula Hoops www.hulahoops.co.uk

Engagingly interactive site from everyone's favourite circular snack.

I Can't Believe It's Not Butter www.tasteyoulove.com

Bit of a tricky one, this. We're assuming that ICBINB's shrive to *luuurve* is supposed to look ultra-cheesy in a cheap Valentine's card type of way – otherwise the design is just plain nasty. Design aside, the content is actually pretty impressive. There's a serialised saga, delivered by e-mail, where you can follow the romantic antics of Samantha by reading her e-diary plus such features as '50 ways to please your lover' and, you've guessed it, plenty of recipes. The content is great but, as for the background, we can't believe it's not better.

Jelly Belly www.jellybelly.com

It's hard not to write something nice about Jelly Belly as their products taste so darn good but, even setting aside our predisposition towards the little gems of confection, this is a superb site, from the history of jelly beans through to a factory tour and even which flavours to mix to get the best out of your beans. Tasty.

Kellogg's www.kelloggs.co.uk

A clumsy layout but it's packed full of Kellogg's news and information, including all of your favourite characters (Coco the monkey and friends) and a superb kids' section. Games, competitions and a community area are backed up with reliable information about nutrition and healthy eating, so you can let your kids have a wander round, safe in the knowledge that they're actually learning something as they go.

Kinder Surprise www.kindersurprise.co.uk

Proving that they're about more than ingenious toys and badly dubbed adverts, Kinder have put a fair amount of effort into creating a site that's both educational and fun. If you have a slow internet connection then you might lose interest before the site has finished loading but, if not, your patience is rewarded with fun, games, Kinder facts and some useful parent and teacher information to keep the grown-ups happy.

Mars www.mars.com

The official site of Mars confectionery and pet food is actually pretty disappointing. Yes, the corporate information is all here but you'd expect something a bit more funky really. The saving grace is the useful links section which takes you to informative sites about some of the confectionery giant's most popular products, from Snickers to Uncle Bens.

Müller www.muller.co.uk

Müller, the yoghurt people, are one of the few European food companies who have invested in a site specifically for the UK market. Having said that, it's not really that surprising when you consider that, according to the site, the company is the number one yoghurt manufacturer in Britain. Plenty of corporate stuff with some consumer information thrown in for good measure. Nothing wrong but nothing special.

Nestlé www.nestle.com

Good idea, Nestlé – who needs fun and cartoon characters when you have a mission statement and an investor relations section?

Quorn www.quorn.com

Why is it that meat-free and organic food sites are so fond of hand-drawn illustrations rather than computer graphics? Quorn's site is surprisingly amateurish when you consider the money behind it but there's some very useful information for mushroom protein lovers if you look hard enough. Needs work, though.

Ryvita www.ryvita.co.uk

Uncluttered and frills-free site from the crunchy snack food. As you'd expect, there are plenty of photos of smiling models enjoying fruit and cheese-topped Ryvita and there's even a Ryvita screensaver if you're *that* bored. The real winner here, though, is the simple but effective height and weight calculator which calculates whether you need to eat less (or more) to stay in shape. Bland but enjoyable – appropriately enough.

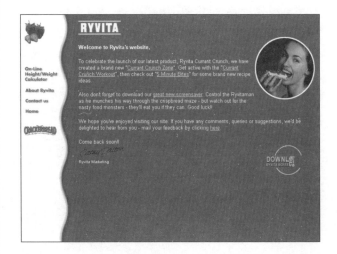

Walkers www.walkers.co.uk

Chester the Cheetah was on hand to welcome us to the Walkers site when we last visited, leading to a mini-site dedicated to the joys of Cheetos. After about half an hour of playing games and taking part in 'Chester's Cheesy Challenge' we finally made it back to the main site which contains everything you ever wanted to know about the company, the products and the promotions (Free Books for Schools etc.). Slick design, fun for the kids and enough hard facts to keep the adults clicking – what more could you ask?

Wotsits www.wotsits.co.uk

Wotsits – everybody's favourite orange snack food, unless you're a rabbit, in which case that would be carrots. Definitively one for the youngsters, who'll have hours of fun clicking on items in Willy's virtual bedroom, playing Cheez-a-roids and generally becoming immersed in Wotsit-mania. Quite possibly the best snack food site on the web. Excellent.

Wrigley's www.wrigley.com

Where are the beautiful people? The romantic chewing gum exchanges? The graphics? Wrigley's may be the chewing gum of choice for consumers across the world but their corporate site couldn't be more dull if it tried. If it wasn't for the 'story of chewing gum' feature, it wouldn't even deserve a mention. Definitely one that's only here for the sake of completeness.

4

healthy eating and diet

Any nutrition or dietary expert will tell you that eating healthily doesn't have to involve starving yourself or even missing out on the foods you enjoy. The internet is packed with sites promising to offer advice on which foods to eat more of, which to cut down on and which are just plain bad for you – from official sites to the online equivalent of old wives' tales, everyone has an opinion. A note of caution, though, be very careful unless you know exactly who's behind a site – as in the real world, it's always a good idea to take medical advice before making drastic dietary changes.

Dieting and weight loss

Trying to shift a few pounds without missing out on meals? Become a slimmer surfer with our guide to the web's best diet and weight loss sites.

■ *The best of the best*

Weightwatchers uk.weightwatchers.com

Weightwatchers may not have the most glossy site on the web but, by all accounts, their healthy eating and diet plans help thousands of people around the world lose weight every year. The site itself contains news, company details, e-mail information about your nearest meeting and even a forum to swap success stories.

◼ The rest of the best

My Nutrition www.mynutrition.co.uk

Plenty of pastel colours (hurray!) on this award-winning 'online guide for everything to do with healthy food, eating and supplements'. News, a free nutrition consultation and expert advice all ensure that you're enjoying a balanced and nutritional diet. Weight Watchers is probably better for dedicated slimmers but if you're trying to live a healthy life, My Nutrition will certainly set you off on the right track.

Diet Sure www.dietsure.com

We can't vouch for the accuracy of the information here, but if it works as well as it seems to then Diet Sure is definitely worth checking out. In a nutshell, you type in information about your diet and lifestyle – either over a period of days or all at once – and the system sends you a full analysis via e-mail within a few hours. It's free and well worth a look.

Nutrition and healthy eating

Healthy eating isn't just about losing weight and there are plenty of online resources to help you ensure that you're getting the right balance between the healthy stuff and the less healthy stuff.

■ The best of the best

British Nutrition Foundation **www.nutrition.org.uk**
The official nature of the BNF site means you can be pretty sure that the information here is going to be accurate. Features dealing with issues as diverse as 'Chinese Healthy Eating' and 'Body Image & Eating Disorders', educational information and foundation news are all well-written and informative but the really useful part is the list of links to relevant informative and educational sites. There's plenty of pictures of fruit too.

■ The rest of the best

Fresh Fruit and Vegetable Information Bureau **www.ffvib.co.uk**
This small but perfectly formed site contains plenty of information about the benefits of a healthy diet of fruit and

vegetables which, it seems, are 'the key to longevity and general all round good health' – but there's more to the site than just earth-shattering revelations, with information about what's in season and even a special mushroom bureau for fungi fans. 'Go for five a day' is the advice from the FFVIB, referring of course to the number of fruit and vegetables you should eat daily. Unfortunately, fruit Polos don't count.

The Nutrition Society www.nutsoc.org.uk

Another grand-sounding name, another stirring mission statement – this lot are 'concerned with the scientific study of nutrition and its application to the maintenance of human and animal health'. This site is aimed at society members and is basically an online version of their twice-yearly gazette, with regularly updated news and features to keep things fresh, although anyone with an interest in healthy eating will find plenty of interesting facts and a discussion forum to meet fellow enthusiasts.

The Food Foundation www.fooddirectory.co.uk

Another great links directory and plenty of information and advice for consumers. The site is sponsored by Marks and Spencer so it looks pretty special and you can't fault the quality of information – uncluttered and functional.

Food Future www.foodfuture.org.uk

Forget the hype and media scare-mongering, for the full low-down on the advantages and disadvantages of genetically modified food, check out this award-winning site from The Food and Drink Federation. Whether you want to know the full background story behind GM or just want a quick overview of whether it can do you any harm, you'll find the answers here. There's more impartial GM debate from *The New Scientist's* GM World site (www.gmworld.newscientist.com).

The Scottish Food and Drink Federation www.sfdf.org.uk

The SFDF promotes the interests of the food and drink manufacturing industry in Scotland, so don't expect much information for consumers. If, however, you're interested in food and drink production, it's a slick enough affair and worth a quick look.

5

wine

Whether you're a sommelier or a purely recreational wine lover, you'll be spoilt for choice when you visit some of our recommended wine sites. For general information or to meet other enthusiasts you'll want to pay a visit to one of the web's extensive wine portals, while for lovers of particular varieties, an increasing number of vineyards are going online to promote their wares. If you want to stock up your cellar, don't forget to check out Chapter 9 Shopping.

Wine portals and information

Your first stop for wine news, information and advice should be one of the portal sites. From British productions like the excellent Wine and Dine (www.winedine.co.uk) to the more international (read: American) Wine Spectator (www.winespectator.com) and Grapevine Weekly (www.grapevineweekly.com), you're bound to find something to suit your tastes.

■ The best of the best

Wine Today www.winetoday.com
Wine Today, from New York Times digital, is unashamedly American in design and content but there's still plenty for

the UK visitor, including some very well-written reviews and advice which won't blind you with jargon. It's not all for enthusiastic amateurs, though – there's a wealth of industry news and event listings, including dates and times of high-profile wine auctions, but the US angle means that it's not overly useful for anyone on this side of the Atlantic. Anything else? Well, you could easily spend hours here checking out the winery listings, advice on matching food and wine, Oz Clarke's wine advice, travel tips, vintage charts, competitions and so much more....

■ *The rest of the best*

Wine Spectator **www.winespectator.com**

Claiming to be 'the most comprehensive wine website in the world' takes some guts. There are hundreds of wine portals on the web, dealing with every conceivable area of wine production and consumption, but when it comes to 'all under one roof' quality, Wine Spectator certainly takes the prize. Wine news, taste tests, cellar secrets, forums, travel information and much more than two years' worth of archive material is available for free, the only downside being that, for the whole Wine Spectator experience, you'll have to pay.

Suite 101 Wine **www.suite101.com/welcome.cfm/wines**

Like About (**www.about.com**), Suite 101 offers a human-edited guide to websites, categorized into hundreds of different subject categories. Their wine category is one of the best in the business with featured articles, website reviews and a discussion forum letting you exchange views with fellow wine buffs. Splendid.

Wine Place **www.wineplace.nu**

A great example of content over design containing everything you ever wanted to know about wine but were too busy drinking it to ask. A guide to wine pronunciations should make it easier to order your favourite 'shato nurf' and a run-down of some common words used to describe wines will make you an instant expert – and there's a whole lot more, including a forum and links to the best of the world *wine* web.

Wine Skinny **www.wineskinny.com**

Ever wondered what wine writers drink in their spare time? No, neither have we but any idle curiosity is more than satisfied by Wine Skinny's imaginatively titled What We Drank this Weekend feature. The popular wine lifestyle magazine also features a whole host of entertaining features to give you the inside track on wine. We like. For a British perspective, try Andrew Jones' excellent Wine on the Web (**www.wineontheweb.co.uk**).

Wine **www.wine.com**

Bit frustrating, this one. If you happen live in America, this is probably the best wine site on the web – the features are excellent, the winery reviews are spot on and the design is excellent. The problem is that Wine.com is, above all else, an online shop, selling a huge variety of wines at more than reasonable prices. Why is that a problem? Well, for those of us who live outside the US, it's just too expensive and too much hassle to place an overseas order, meaning that we can look but we can't taste – like a child outside a closed sweetshop. Worth checking out for the features, though.

Grapevine Weekly **www.grapevineweekly.com**

Well-presented links to articles from some of the web's most impressive wine magazines. Wine Today (see above) is featured along with The Wine News (**www.thewinenews.com**), Wine Pocket List (**www.winepocketlist.com**), Wine Brats (**www.winebrats.org**) and the wonderfully off-beat Wine X Wired (**www.winexwired.com**).

■ *The best of the rest*

Daily Wine **www.dailywine.com**

Fresh and funky site featuring a wine of the day, a wine of the month and a smattering of well-written features.

Wine Online www.wineonline.co.uk

In terms of design, Wine Online (which rhymes) doesn't really shine. However, there's a mixed bag of features, including news, information, event reviews and links to other interesting food and drink sites – some of which are well worth looking at. It's British too!

Wine Authority www.wineauthority.com

Despite the official-sounding title, this site doesn't belong to the wine police – instead it's the number one source for fine wine reviews from the Napa Valley. Apparently.

Vineyards and regions

From California's Napa Valley to Cornwall's Camel Valley, we're living in a whole world of wine. Whatever region produces your favourite variety, you can find out everything you need to know about the countries, regions and individual vineyards using our handy guide to the world's wine producers.

■ *The best of the best*

French Wines and Food www.frenchwinesfood.com

As the name suggests, this site is about more than just wine but the guide to reds, whites and champagne is certainly a major attraction. A quick run-down of the different varieties and vintages is complemented by a vintage chart, classification information and some well-chosen French wine links to the rest of the web – all with a superb design making everything a joy to use. *Très bon*.

■ *The rest of the best*

The German Wine Page **www.winepage.de**

Unlike its French counterpart, the German Wine Page hasn't wasted any time on design. The no-frills but easy-to-browse layout makes it easy to find the information you need, from an introduction to the mysteries of the wine label to a (very) brief history of German wine and even some useful taste notes.

The Spanish Wine Page **vino.eunet.es/vino**

Like the German Wine Page, this excellent Spanish site started life way back in 1995 and has gone from strength to strength since. All the usual guides to regions, vineyards and vintages are here as well some useful information on Spanish cuisine in general. Check out the links section for more of the same.

English Wine www.english-wine.com

English wine may not have a great reputation but if the information here is anything to go by, it's fast increasing in both popularity and quality. The history of English and Welsh wine production, a guide to vineyards and even an explanation of the surprising difference between English and British wine – it's all on this down-to-earth site.

■ The best of the rest

Moet & Chandon www.moet.com

The official site from one of the world's leading Champagne producers.

Still looking? Check out the Good Cooking Wine Link Page (www.goodcooking.com/wwinelnk.htm) for more wine production regions.

Wine making and selling

Fancy making your own wine? Where better to look for hints, tips and general expert advice than on the world's greatest reference tool. As you'd expect, the web is packed full of useful resources for both budding and experienced wine makers so there's no reason why you can't produce your very own award-winning wine vintage – except perhaps the British weather.

■ The best of the best

Viticulture www.viticulture.co.uk

Launched in 1999, this useful site aims to serve the United Kingdom's grape-growing and wine-making community –

both professional and amateur – though step-by-step guides, tricks and hints, a forum, and suppliers' directory. If you're planning on starting your own vineyard, it's certainly a great place to start.

advice, information, services, supplies, news, discussion...

INDEX:
Click on under-lined items to select

On-line Forum - exchange views, share problems, seek/give advice - it's easy to use - try it now!

Winegrowers Supplies
Visit Derek Pritchard's webpage for quality vines and vineyard and winery equipment

Notes on viticulture
Useful hints for newcomers to grape growing

Buying a vineyard
Points to remember when pursuing that dream!

Trade Directory
Helping you to find the equipment or services you need

Small Ads

This website was launched on 9 December 1999. It aims to serve the United Kingdom's grape-growing and wine-making community - both professional and amateur.

Contributions wanted! Share your knowledge and experience with other growers - articles, comments, views, experience, memories - we want them. Either use our on-line forum (see index in left-hand column) or e-mail your contribution to webmaster@viticulture.co.uk, fax to +44 (0)24 7667 9099 or post to Viticulture-UK, 37 Warwick Avenue, Coventry, CV5 6DJ, United Kingdom.

Latest News: Let us have your news! Whether you are a vineyard owner, winemaker or supplier to the industry, tell us your news. If it is news for English wine consumers we will post it on *www.english-wine.com* our website aimed at the consumer market. If it is news for the english winegrowing and winemaking industry we'll post it on this website - same day in both cases. **This**

Have you visited our sister-site www.english-wine.com which is aimed at consumers (and potential consumers) of English wine?

Already, thousands are visiting www.english-wine.com each month and it is already at the top of the key search engines' rankings. **Your vineyard can be listed FREE OF CHARGE on www.english-wine.com in our directory of English vineyards.**

Or, for a fee, you can have a fuller entry (with photo), a full webpage about your vineyard or even your own full website.

We also offer links to your website if you already have one.

Send us your details for your free listing now (vineyard name, name of owner(s) and address, telephone number, acreage of

■ The rest of the best

Smart Wine Online **www.smartwine.com**

Essential bookmark for anyone working in the wine industry. There's news for growers, distributors, sellers (and cellars) and links to some of the best sources of market trends and analysis to keep your finger on the pulse.

spirits and cocktails

Wine lovers are not the only ones catered for on the web. If you prefer the grain to the grape then you'll find cocktail recipes galore as well as official and unofficial tributes to the individual spirits themselves. Just make sure you don't get carried away otherwise you may end up paying a visit to **www.alcoholics-anonymous.org.uk**.

Spirits

Before you dive into the exciting world of cocktails, you might want to find out a little more about the raw materials themselves. Most of the major spirit companies have their own official sites and there are even some 'fan' sites dedicated to the cooler brands like Jack Daniels and Absolut Vodka (e.g. **www.absolutcollectors.com**), meaning that no matter what your tipple of choice is, you're bound to find something to suit.

Absolut Vodka **www.absolutvodka.com**
Famous for their innovative advertising campaigns, many of which have become collectors' items. Oh, and they make Vodka too. Absolut class.

Bacardi www.bacardi.com

Aged with passion since 1862. Includes a screensaver, recipes and a rather threatening set of terms and conditions which pop up when you first arrive. What more could you want?

Baileys www.baileys.com

Smooth, slick and sexy in parts, a bit clumsy in others. Welcome to the Baileys Pleasure Dome indeed.

Captain Morgan www.rum.com

Playing the sex card in the most blatant of ways, Captain Morgan uses huge pictures of attractive models in order to entice you into the site. Once in, though, you can support Captain Morgan's campaign for president. Gets our vote.

Drambuie www.drambuie.co.uk

One of the few spirit brands to have a UK version of their site. The design is suitably dark and moody with downloads, animations and the ever-gripping Drambuie story.

Famous Grouse www.famousgrouse.com
It's famous but there are no grouse in it. Any site with a village shop and post office is alright by us.

Finlandia Vodka www.finlandia-vodka.com
Uncluttered, hip and no attempt to prevent children from entering – that'll please the parents.

Glenfiddich www.glenfiddich.com
Impressive site, heavy on company news, light on fun.

Glenmorangie www.glenmorangie.com
Let Glenmorangie's 'glen of tranquillity' take you on a journey of discovery through a world of whisky.

Grand Marnier www.grand-marnier.com
Slightly bizarre layout but a not unimpressive effort.

J & B www.jbscotch.com
An 'in your face' site from the whisky giant. A bit slow to load but well worth the wait.

Jack Daniels www.jackdaniels.com
Jack Daniels are clearly working hard to make this site accessible to as many people as possible, with translations into Japanese and Brazilian. The design is as good as you'd expect from such a cool brand and, if you're a Jack Daniels drinker, there's plenty to see.

Jim Beam www.jimbeam.com
The Jim Beam site asks you for your date of birth before you can enter and assuming you're of legal drinking age, you'll find yourself in the Jim Bean virtual bar featuring

company information, a jukebox and even a talent spotter for up and coming bands. Well worth a browse.

Johnnie Walker www.scotch.com

Memorable address, memorable site. Red, black, gold and blue label are featured with a slick backdrop and plenty of product information.

Laphroaig www.laphroaig.com

Arty site featuring a forum, product info and lots more. You can even register for your free plot of land on the island of Islay.

Smirnoff www.smirnoff.com

One of the most impressive spirit sites, featuring a cocktail generator, e-mail postcards, product history and the ever-entertaining Planet Smirnoff.

Southern Comfort www.southerncomfort.com

Enjoy the spirit of New Orleans with events, recipes, merchandise and the usual product history.

Tia Maria www.tiamaria.co.uk

Feed your mind, body and spirit with short but sweet features on aromatherapy, tarot, voodoo and more.

Cocktails

Let's face it – cocktails are cool. James Bond wouldn't have been half as suave had he sauntered up to the bar and ordered an orange juice, and it wouldn't have done Tom Cruise's career any good to have starred in the film

'Cordial'. So grab your stirrers and stock up on little paper umbrellas, it's time to explore the best cocktail sites on the web. For more cocktail tips and tricks, check out some of the larger food and drink portals in Chapter 2.

■ The best of the best

iDrink www.drink.com

Simply tell this superb site which ingredients you have at home – from apple juice to absinth – and it will suggest a range of cocktails that you can try. The database system looks simple enough but is, in fact, extremely fast and accurate, allowing you to search through thousands of recipes in seconds – and if your favourite isn't listed, you can make it available for other users to try. Obviously the site is aimed at people of legal drinking age but if you want something with less of a kick, you can 'switch' the alcoholic recipes off – a nice touch on an excellent site.

■ *The rest of the best*

Webtender www.webtender.com

Webtender – bartender, geddit? Never mind. This massive directory site provides a thorough guide to the best cocktail recipes, drink retailers and general-interest sites on the web. The design is not particularly inspiring but if you want a quick way to find what you're looking for, it's hard to beat.

Cocktail Times www.cocktailtimes.com

Time for a cocktail? This very nice-looking site features recipes, news, advice and information aplenty. The cocktail list may not be quite as impressive as iDrink but the presentation is superb, with a clear list of ingredients, illustrations and brief but adequate directions. Once you've finished testing out the recipes (in, say, five or six months) there's a whole world of other cocktail information, including the inside track on bartending, glassware, party planning and the history of cocktails. Nice.

Cocktail hotwired.lycos.com/cocktail

Proving that there's more to Lycos than searching for MP3s and pictures of Pamela Anderson, their excellent cocktail resource provides a drink of the week, well-stocked recipe archive, tips on mixing and the inspirational Virtual Blender which gives ideas on what to make next.

Cocktail.com www.cocktail.com

A slightly confusing mix of cocktail recipes, industry news and shopping. If you're heavily into the cocktail scene, you'll probably find plenty here but, for everyone else, you're probably better to stick to Cocktail Times or iDrink.

7

beer

Aaaah, beer – the alcoholic workhorse – no ice, no straws and definitely no fancy umbrellas. Whether you prefer the designer American varieties or good old-fashioned real ale, there's something for everyone in our guide to the best beer, lager, bitter and ale sites on the web. For pubs and bars, flip to the imaginatively titled Pubs and bars section in Chapter 10.

Guides and portals

As with most things on the web, you don't have to spend hours dredging through search engines to find the best beer sites. Simply check out some of our recommended guides and portal sites.

■ *The best of the best*

Breworld **www.breworld.com**

It's not often that the best site in a particular category hails from the UK but, in the case of the Staines-based Breworld, there really is no competition. Beer news, city guides, trade directories, discussion groups and, just in case you still can't find what you're looking for, there's more links than you could shake a pint at. So much beer, so little time.

■ The rest of the best

Beer Site www.beersite.com

Looking for beer sites? Look no further than the number one beer search site on the web – a kind of Ya-brew if you will. From e-zines to official publications, it's all sorted, sifted and categorised for your browsing pleasure.

Beer www.beer.com

American site which proves that beer is more than just a drink, it's a way of life. Music, entertainment, live events, fun stuff and even the occasional mention of beer make this a pretty impressive way to waste a few hours. Be warned though, the site has a bit of a lad's mag feel so it's probably suitable for adults only – a bit like beer really.

Real Beer www.realbeer.com

Unashamedly American site claiming to offer everything you could ever want to know about beer, brewpubs, microbreweries, home brewing, and the beer industry. While that might not be quite true (unless you refuse to acknowledge anything outside the States), there's certainly lots to see and do. News, features, a brewery guide, a library and an impressive links list make this well worth a quick click.

The Campaign for Real Ale www.camra.org.uk

The Campaign for Real Ale's home on the internet has one goal – to convince you that good old-fashioned British beers and ciders are the way forward. Regardless of where you stand on this contentious issue, the site is extremely well put together with information about the various real ales, campaign news, plenty of persuasive prose and the excellent Good Beer Guide listing thousands of real ale pubs around the UK. Fed up of bland chemical-filled beers? This could be your idea of heaven. For more of the same, try the Real Ale Guide (www.real-ale-guide.co.uk).

Bar Meister www.barmeister.com

You might not think you need an 'online guide to drinking' as most people are pretty good at drinking without any help. However, this engaging site deals with everything other than the act itself, including drinking games, forums, cocktail recipes and, when we visited, a poll on the burning question of whether 'wine sucks'. Definitely not one for the wine buff.

The Absolute Authority on Beer www.absoluteauthority.com/beer

This modestly titled affair features links to forums, mailing lists, advice and a whole load of other community-orientated stuff. Not exactly authoritative but well worth a look nonetheless.

Breweries

As with the major spirit brands, it's not really possible to choose a best of the best – it depends on your personal taste but, if you don't have a favourite and just want to find an impressive site, check out the excellent snail race and screensavers from Guinness (www.guiness.com) – otherwise, read on for our A–Z of the best brewers on the web.

Amstel www.amstel.com

A shrine to football, Amsterdam and even the occasional mention of beer on this overwhelmingly red site.

Bass www.bass-brewers.com

A definite corporate feel on the official site of Bass' brewing arm. Although the 'Odds and Sods' section sounded promising, it's all just a bit formal. For even more about Bass, visit their main site (www.bass.com).

Becks www.becks-beer.com

Futuristic site containing lots of promotional information about Becks' Formula 1 interests. Look out for Becks Futures, a gallery of work for up and coming artists with a total prize of £65,000 for the best.

Boddingtons www.boddingtons.com

Boddingtons' recent Graham and Claudia promotion (the cartoon cow and the cartoon babe) is carried over to their online marketing with this fun and funky official site. There's a screensaver, a strangely addictive game, stills from the TV ads and – if you're the sort of person who has posters of Lara Croft on your wall – you'll love the downloadable Claudia desktop pics.

Budweiser www.budweiser.com

The official Budweiser site starts by asking your 'born on date' (perhaps 'date of birth' would be better?) but grammatical quibbles aside, the self-proclaimed King of Beers has done pretty well here. As you might expect, there's an American blokey feel about the whole thing, with live web chats with famous models to keep you coming back for more, but there's also plenty of product info and the design is suitably cool so it's hard to complain. If you're looking for the traditional Czech Budweiser Budvar, look no further than www.budweiser.cz.

Carlsberg www.carlsberg.co.uk

A fun-packed site complete with games, music, football, screensavers, promotions and special events. Even if you don't drink Carlsberg, this is an essential visit.

Cobra www.cobrabeer.com

The curry lover's beer of choice has opted for the usual mix of competitions, info and postcards with an off-beat, vindaloo-stained design for their official site.

Fosters www.fostersbeer.com

You could never accuse Fosters of forgetting their Australian roots if this kangaroo and barbecue-filled site is anything to go by. It even allows you to lobby for boomerang throwing to be acknowledged as an Olympic sport. Strewth.

Grolsch www.grolsch.com

A slightly confusing layout but plenty of stuff for Grolsch fans, including a nifty movie matrix and product information on their range of premium beers.

Guinness www.guiness.ie

Snail racing, downloadable screensavers, classic advertisements and clean innovative design. Pure genius.

Heineken www.heineken.com

Click on the popping bubbles of Heineken to navigate your way around this slick array of games, information, chat rooms, travel and much, much more.

Kronenbourg www.kronenbourg1664.co.uk

Suitably dark and funky site extolling the virtues of Kronenbourg.

Labatts www.labatt.com

This thoroughly US-orientated site requires you to register in order to take full advantage of the features on offer – but it's free so you can't really complain.

Scrumpy Jack www.scrumpyjack.com

The official pint of the English Cricket Team – and obviously very proud of it. Cricket fans go here now.

Shepherd Neame www.shepherd-neame.co.uk

Britain's oldest brewer presents one of Britain's strangest navigation systems.

Thwaites www.thwaites.co.uk

According to the opening blurb – 'this site was designed with the future in mind'. That may well be the case but the design still feels a little last century – and it's all a bit too corporatey.

8

soft drinks

The web may have thousands of alcohol-related sites but non-alcoholic favourites are pretty well represented too. From tea to Tizer, it's all here.

Tea and coffee

Tea and coffee have fewer sites on the internet than, say, cocktails and beer but don't worry – there's more than enough caffeinated content online to keep you buzzing 'til the early hours.

■ The best of the best

Smell the Coffee **www.smellthecoffee.com**
The design may not be overly inspiring but these people certainly know their coffee. Forums, well-written articles and an almost evangelical belief in the power of the coffee bean make this a thoroughly entertaining read – and the directory will ensure that you're never more than a couple of clicks away from espresso enlightenment.

■ *The rest of the best*

Tea Health www.teahealth.co.uk

This official site from the UK Tea Council (yes, there is a UK Tea Council) concentrates on the benefits of tea for a healthy lifestyle. On top of an array of facts and figures to support the argument that tea is the cure for all ailments, there is an impressive amount of information about the beverage itself, including production methods, varieties, its history and – for medical professionals – downloadable information for patients. There's also a nice photograph of a happy couple running across a beach, presumably after enjoying a nice cup of tea. For their main site check out Tea (www.tea.co.uk).

Koffee Korner www.koffeekorner.com

Culture, health trivia, features, cartoons and enough koffee-related kontent to keep you kontent for a considerable amount of time. Less of the same at The Coffee Club (www.coffee.co.uk).

Tea Time www.teatime.com

Not as feature-packed as Tea Health but this useful resource is full of interesting tea facts and quotes – and there are regular chat sessions to discuss the finer points of the subject.

Tea and Coffee www.teaandcoffee.net

If you have a professional interest in the tea and coffee industries, this is an essential bookmark. Industry news, current affairs and features are the main ingredients but there's also a message centre, calendar of events, up-to-the-minute information ticker and some sharp editorial content which will even appeal to non-industry types.

Fizzy drinks

Generally speaking, soft drink sites tend to be more impressive than their alcoholic counterparts. Perhaps this is because of the large number of young people the sites attract or perhaps soft drink companies are more interested in the web. Whatever the reason, there are hours of fun in store for you on some of our favourite sites and, for the inside track on carbonated beverages, check out the fascinating Soda Fountain (www.sodafountain.com).

■ The best of the best

Coca Cola www.cocacola.com

You would expect a huge company like Coke to have sussed the web from day one but it actually took them a ridiculous amount of time to get to this stage. Following a recent makeover, what was once a bizarre and unfocused attempt at online promotion has become one of the sharpest, coolest sites on the web. From downloadable polar bears to fresh and funky tunes, the site has something for everyone and, as for the quality of design, it's impossible to fault. Enjoy.

■ The rest of the best

Pepsi www.pepsi.co.uk

Far be it from us to accuse Pepsi of trying to buy popularity but they do seem to have shelled out a few quid on getting top names to endorse the black fizzy stuff. When we last visited, it was Robbie Williams and David Beckham but by the time you get there they'll have probably chosen another star du jour to add sex appeal. Cynicism aside, the site is very well put together with a futuristic theme and uncluttered design but, be warned, it can take a while to load, so it's probably a good idea to go and make a cup of tea while the site is getting itself together.

Irn Bru www.irn-bru.co.uk

The undisputed winner of our 'wasting time when you should be working' award, the Irn Bru site is filled with downloads and gimmicks to wind up your friends and waste your workday. From mini games to spoof e-mails, there's plenty to try out, our particular favourite being the automated robot chat thing that lets you chat to yourself for hours... and hours... and hours. Superb.

Tango www.tango.co.uk

Tango are renowned for their innovative advertising and bizarre free gifts – and their official site doesn't let the side down. Watch the latest TV advert, download the characters, find out about Gotan and generally spend hours exploring this addictively brilliant (and brilliantly addictive) site. Well done Tango.

Tizer www.tizer.co.uk

Tizer's recent increase in popularity may have come as
something of a shock to those of us who remember it first
time around but, as this site demonstrates, new Tizer is so
much cooler than before. Like so many soft drink sites, the
emphasis here is on music, with exclusive tracks, a cus-
tomised version of Winamp (www.winamp.com) and plenty
more besides. Rock 'n' roll.

Lucozade www.lucozade.co.uk

Another drink which has recently become cool again,
Lucozade has produced an extremely impressive site to
promote both the classic energy drink and the new and
exciting Solstis. As you might expect, the emphasis here is
on energy, and with pumped-up section titles like 'mega
blast' and 'dynamo' it does tread the fine line between naff
and hip at times but, all in all, it's well worth a look if you're
feeling run down.

Virgin Cola www.virgincola.co.uk

Sir Rick once claimed that his brand of cola would outsell
the big two companies in the UK market. Hmmm. Ok, so it
isn't quite as popular as R.B would like it to be but the official Virgin Cola site is certainly capable of mixing it with
the best of them. The smart 'n' sassy Roller Girl welcomes
you into a world of fun and excitement and there's certainly
enough to keep you occupied for a while including music,
discounts, competitions and product info. We like.

Dr Pepper www.drpepper.com

Their TV ads may be funny but Dr Peppers' official site
takes itself a little too seriously for our tastes. Blatant prod-

uct shots and plenty of content for American visitors do very little to impress UK folk but, fortunately, the day is saved by a superb and addictive little racing game.

Evian www.evian.com

This pastel-coloured site is definitely aimed at female consumers, with links to women's fashion and health sitting alongside the usual mix of music, competitions and product blurb. Worth visiting just for the screensaver. More of the same from Perrier (www.perrier.com) and Volvic (www.volvic.co.uk).

9

shopping

Whether you fancy a bar of chocolate or hunger for a gourmet meal, you'll be more than satisfied with the rich and varied selection of food and drink available on the web. Organic produce, fine wines, fresh fruit and all the rest of your weekly shopping can now be delivered directly to your door, leaving you even more time to slave over a hot stove. Or not.

Supermarkets

Posting a pork pie causes problems. This simple truth resulted in a slightly shaky start for online food and drink sales in the UK, with companies struggling to arrange reliable and affordable methods of delivery. Obviously there are some products like hampers, cheese, chocolate and coffee which can be sent through the post or delivered by courier but sending your weekly shopping is not quite so easy. Fortunately, thanks largely to companies such as Iceland (www.iceland.co.uk) and Tesco (www.tesco.co.uk), British shoppers have taken in droves to the idea of having their shopping delivered, encouraging these companies (and more) to invest some serious money in rolling the service out nationwide. The non-city dwellers amongst us may still have to rely on traditional supermarkets for a while yet but no matter where you live, it's never been easier to get stuffed.

■ *The best of the best*

Tesco www.tesco.co.uk

Tesco may not have delivery quite as sussed as Iceland but their range of products, customer service and ease of use is the best in the business. If you live within one of the growing number of Tesco delivery areas, it's simply a case of registering on the site, choosing your items and waiting for

a shiny delivery van to arrive with your weekly shopping. Naturally you are going to get situations where something you order isn't in stock, in which case you get the chance to opt for an alternative product. It's not just about food and drink, though – you can also buy books, music, gifts and even personal finance services. If this excellent service covered the whole of the UK there'd be no need to leave your house again. Well done Tesco.

■ The rest of the best

Iceland www.iceland.co.uk

Mum may have gone to Iceland in an old advertising campaign but thanks to Iceland's excellent home shopping service, she can stay home and put her feet up. An impressive range of groceries are available for delivery to an impressive 97% of the UK and as long as you spend over £40 you won't pay any extra for the service. When it comes to the number of products, Tesco and Sainsbury's are slightly better stocked but if you don't live in a major city – Iceland's home delivery is a godsend.

Sainsbury's www.sainsburys.co.uk

Like Tesco, Sainsbury's home delivery service is only available to those lucky people who live in a restricted delivery area but if you are fortunate enough to be eligible you can call upon the services of a team of specially trained shoppers to do your shopping for you. The site itself is very well thought out and there are some nice touches in the shopping system itself – such as allowing you to specify what size potatoes you want or how ripe you like your plums.

■ The best of the rest

Aldi www.aldi-stores.co.uk

Find your nearest store or even a new job with the official UK site of the German supermarket giant. Cheap and cheerful is the name of the game here, but there's no online ordering so you're going to have to get in the car.

Asda www.asda.co.uk

If Asda's web presence was the film *Twins* and Value mad is Arnold Schwarzenegger then their main information site is very definitely Danny DeVito. Functional but not superb.

Budgens www.budgens.co.uk

Save time. Save money. Shop Budgens – that's the message from the pretty slick official site of the low-cost supermarket chain. There's no fully featured online ordering yet but if you live near a store and don't mind paying over £50, you can order a limited selection of products over the web. Nice.

Co-op www.co-op.co.uk

Everything you could possibly need to know about the stores, the philosophy, the staff and the products. Whether you're a Co-op member or just a regular shopper, you'll learn something here.

Safeway www.safeway.co.uk

No online ordering yet but Safeway shoppers will enjoy the recipes, news and information on this extremely slick site.

Waitrose **www.waitrose.com**
Not as well stocked as the top dogs but the online ordering
is well worth checking out if you usually shop at Waitrose.

Speciality food

Bored with beans? Tired of toast? If you're looking for a
taste of the exotic, you'll find a wealth of speciality food
shops waiting to take your order online. From organic food
to fine wines, gourmet cheeses to smoked hams – it's all
here. Tuck in.

■ The best of the best

Teddington Cheese **www.teddingtoncheese.co.uk**
When you feel cheesy there's only one place to come for
over 130 varieties of the nation's favourite cracker topping.
It's not just cheese, though – crackers, chutneys and hampers are also available along with book offers and a free
cheese-filled newsletter. Teddington Cheese may be a small
company but its no-frills site is capable of taking on all
comers with its huge range, stress-free ordering and refreshingly friendly service. How cheese would want to be sold.

■ The rest of the best

Organics Direct **www.organicsdirect.com**
An award-winning and environmentally friendly site offering fruit, veg, pasta, baby food, bread, cakes and plenty
more. The prices aren't cheap (although there's a 5 per cent

Welcome to The Teddington Cheese Online

At our shop we specialise in cheese produced on small farms using traditional methods. Cheeses from all over Britain and Europe are matured on our premises, then cut and served when in peak condition. Over 130 different varieties are currently available and we continue to enjoy searching for new discoveries.

British and Continental Cheesemongers

Our new shopping basket system has been introduced to help you choose and order from our extensive range.

ENTER

© The Teddington Cheese

discount for regular orders) but you're buying into a set of ideals – everything is certified organic (and GM free), all of the growers are guaranteed a fair deal and the quality is second to none. Ordering is a little complicated but it's free if you buy enough. Excellent.

The Fresh Food Co. www.freshfood.co.uk

Claiming to be 'Britain's original, biggest and fastest online organic shopping service', the Fresh Food Co. certainly has an impressive enough site. Everything is laid out in a sensible way, making it easy to browse, and the list of comments from satisfied customers should be more than enough to persuade you to start shopping.

Blue Mango www.bluemango.co.uk

It loads slowly and has a stupid name but the range of food offered by this online grocery store is nothing short of impressive. Chutneys, confectionery, curds, dips and salsas, gifts, honey and sauces, jams, marmalades, mustards, flavoured sauces, teas and so much more make Blue Mango one of the most tempting stores on the web.

Clearwater Hampers www.hamper.com

If you prefer to buy your food by the basketful, this is definitely the site for you. Some extremely tasty-sounding hampers are available here, packed with port, stilton, smoked salmon and other gourmet treats and if you can't find exactly what you're looking for you can even create your own. Ideal gifts for people who have everything. For more of the same try 800 Hampers (www.800hampers.com).

French Hampers www.frenchhampers.co.uk

As the name suggests, this is a great place to find traditional French foods either as gifts or for your own personal consumption. They're not cheap, with prices starting at £100 – and going up to £10,000 (!) – but the quality of food is excellent and the Which? Web Trader logo guarantees a stress-free ordering experience.

Fortnum and Mason www.fortnumandmason.co.uk

More hampers to be found here plus a nice range of chocolates, wine and gifts. The site may be user-friendly but the prices are strictly for the well heeled. Expensive, but remember – you get what you pay for. Almost.

Gourmet World www.gourmet-world.co.uk

Top-quality gourmet meals delivered straight to your door – ideal for lazy food lovers or for when you want to impress someone by passing it off as your own. From Polentina cake to risotto, burgundy to claret, it's not cheap but it's mouth-wateringly tempting.

Sweet Mart www.sweetmart.co.uk

Before you get too carried away, we should point out that this isn't the place to come for fruit gums and aniseed balls. The Bristol Sweet Mart specialises in supplying ethnic foods and spices to the general public and to the restaurant trade and, judging by the excellent range on their website, you shouldn't have too much trouble finding the one you're looking for. The prices seem reasonable and ordering couldn't be easier.

Thorntons www.thorntons.co.uk

You already know the Thorntons product range – chocolate, fudge, toffee and assorted chewy things. Their slightly cluttered site is a great way to send your loved one a few extra calories and once you've spent a few minutes on the site you'll probably want to place an order for personal consumption as well. For those with entrepreneurial tendencies there's also information about setting up a Thorntons franchise. Tasty.

◼ The best of the rest

Heinz Direct www.heinz-direct.co.uk

It may not be Fortnum and Mason but Heinz have done well with this tins by mail service. The delivery can take up to a month but if you don't mind waiting for your beans and baby food – it does the job.

Lobster **www.lobster.co.uk**

Luxury foods aplenty on this appropriately luxurious site. Caviar and champagne, fois gras and pastries and, surprise surprise, there's even a range of hampers. If you enjoy your food and don't mind paying a few quid for the best – that's what you'll get here.

Drink

Perhaps it's a question of profit or maybe internet users are all a bunch of boozers but it's much easier to buy alcohol online than it is to buy soft drinks. Oh well, if you can put up with the inconvenience of being forced to drink alcohol rather than mineral water you'll be spoilt for choice on our recommended virtual off-licences.

■ *The best of the best*

Chateau Online **www.chateauonline.co.uk**

Welcome to wine lovers' heaven. Chateau Online combines an excellent range of wine with expert advice from a top sommelier so you can be sure that you're getting the best, and with bases in France, Germany and Ireland as well as the UK site you're certainly not dealing with a fly-by-night operation. Even if you don't want to make a purchase, you'll find plenty to do on the site, with forums and advice on how to set up a cellar and match the right food to the right wine. Ordering, as you've probably guessed, is simplicity itself and there's a flat-rate delivery charge of £5.99 so it's well worth stocking up. If you're looking for a bottle of a particular rare vintage, check out Wine Searcher (**www.winesearcher.com**).

■ *The rest of the best*

Last Orders **www.lastorders.com**

Ok, so Chateau Online may have the wine market sewn up but what if you fancy a beer? Last Orders is the UK's leading online off-licence offering a massive range of beers, lagers, spirits, soft drinks and, yes, there's some wine too. The site is a joy to use with everything laid out in a logical order and the prices won't break the bank either. Although delivery is extremely prompt, it's a good idea to plan ahead if you're organising a weekend drinking session – if you order during the week you can take advantage of free delivery directly to your door. Very nice.

Amivin www.amivin.com

If over 4000 wines available for immediate delivery isn't enough to impress you, the range of extra features offered by Amivin certainly will be. Wine buffs will be pleased at how easy it is to navigate straight to a particular vintage but if you do need a little advice, Amivin's experts will be glad to point you in the right direction. There's also a number of excellent promotions, a gift wizard and a wine lovers' club. From everyday wines to the finest of the fine – you'll be spoilt for choice.

Now 365 www.now365.com

Although not quite as sharp as the superb Last Orders, this site is still pretty special. The usual range of beer, wines and spirits are here along with a selection of soft drinks and, if you're worried about making sure your alcohol arrives safely, you'll be pleased to see the familiar Which? Web Trader logo.

Drinks Direct www.drinks-direct.co.uk

Uncluttered and simple to navigate, Drinks Direct will deliver your favourite tipple directly to your door within two working days. Delivery costs £5.99 per order, so it's worth ordering a few bottles at once to spread the cost – and while you're ordering, why not check out their range of flowers and chocolates, ideal for the special someone in your life.

Whisky Shop www.whiskyshop.com

That's right, it's a shop that sells whisky. Malts, rare, blended, liqueurs, half bottles and even miniatures (no more stealing from hotel mini-bars) ensure that no matter how much of which type of whisky you're after, you'll be spoilt for choice here.

Shopwine **www.shopwine.co.uk**

The name says it all. If you are shopping for wine you'll find an exceptional range on offer, categorised by style, country and price, while spirit lovers will definitely want to check out the site's Spirit Vault which contains a superb range of brandies and malt whiskies as well as all of the traditional favourites. A Which? Web Trader member.

Extras

Ok, so you've sorted out the food and drink but what about the extra bits and pieces you need, like crockery, cutlery, glassware, pots, pans and tablecloths? Don't worry – we've thought of that too.

Directories and department stores

Although there are plenty of specialist retailers happy to take your hard earned cash in exchange for the very latest table and kitchenware, you can often get a better deal by shopping around on one of the web's big directory sites and department stores.

■ *The best of the best*

Kelkoo **www.kelkoo.com**

Another site which proves that the best internet companies are the ones with the silly names (Google? Yahoo?). Kelkoo is a truly global shop comparison site and, although some countries are better represented than others, over 25,000 merchants from around the world are listed. If you've got plenty of time on your hands you can browse the entire directory yourself but it's much quicker to use the auto-mated comparison system to sniff out the best price on books, music, films, games, computers, wine, electronics, toys, flights and a whole range of other stuff. Before you spend any money on the internet, make sure you shop around with this invaluable resource.

■ *The best of the rest*

2020 Shops www.2020shops.com

While Kelkoo is the online shopper's most powerful weapon, 2020 Shops is like a well-informed best mate. Other sites are busy developing automated shopping robots and search tools but this directory is trying to give internet shopping a friendly face. What really makes 2020 Shops stand out from the crowd is not their huge range of features (there's a definite lack of gimmicks) but rather the quality of the site reviews which have been written by professional journalists and are refreshingly honest and to the point. Whether you're buying a salt cellar or a saucepan, a quick visit to this excellent site will get you on the right track in no time.

Great Universal www.greatuniversal.co.uk

The online arm of Great Universal Stores (GUS) doesn't fail to impress with this mammoth site. If you already have one of their paper catalogues you can use the online order form to speed things up or if you're a first-time visitor it's simple enough to browse through their incredible range of products. From nightwear to nit combs, boxer shorts to football kits, it's all here and with years of mail order experience you can expect great customer service and prompt delivery. Proof that traditional companies can make a killing on the web. *Huuuuge.*

Specialist suppliers

If you simply couldn't serve food on anything less than Spode china, you're probably going to need to part with a few quid. Fortunately, the following sites are always happy to oblige.

■ The best of the best

Scott & Sargeant Cookshop www.scottsargeant.com

Scott and Sargeant claim to be the most comprehensive collection of cookware, giftware and tableware on the internet – and they may well be right! From Le Creuset saucepans to Gaggia coffee machines, all the big brands are here, along with everything else you could need for both the kitchen and the dining room – all at pretty reasonable prices. Like a who's who of kitchen and tableware.

■ The rest of the best

Spode www.spode.co.uk

If it's high-quality china you're after, you need look no further than this excellent site from Spode. Although at
present you can't order directly online, there's a complete
list of stockists so it shouldn't be too hard to track the stuff
down after you've chosen from the huge range on the site.
According to this site, Josiah Spode was responsible for the
creation of fine bone china in 1800 – despite the slight
handicap of having died in 1797. Now that's dedication.

Royal Doulton www.royal-doulton.com

If you need an introduction to Royal Doulton, you
probably can't afford it anyway. This slightly sparse, but
informative nonetheless, site features details of the range,
availability information and all of the aloofness you would
expect. We're not worthy. Apparently.

restaurants, pubs, bars and takeaways

Don't fancy slaving away in the kitchen? Why not let some-one else take the strain by eating out or ordering a takeaway? Alternatively, if you fancy a pint, the web can help you out too.

Restaurants

You might wonder what use the internet can be when making wining and dining arrangements. Well, other than the obvious advantage of being able to check out a restaurant before you arrive using one the of the popular review and rating sites such as the AA's restaurant guide (**www.theaa.co.uk**), an increasing number of sites allow you to book tables at some of the UK's top eating establishments.

■ The best of the best

AA Restaurant and Hotel Guide www.theaa.co.uk
Over 8000 hotels and restaurants are featured in the com-prehensive searchable guide to UK eateries. Simply choose

the region, price band, and quality of food you are looking for, and you'll instantly be offered a list of options – every one reviewed in detail by the AA. The presentation is spot on and with the huge range of other features available on the site, it would be crazy not to visit at least once. Well done the AA.

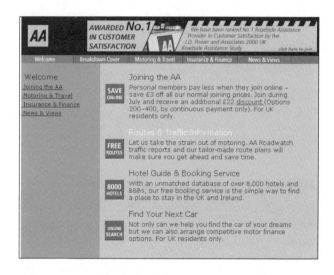

■ The rest of the best

Restaurants www.restaurants.co.uk

Another huge directory of restaurants across the UK, featuring brief details of over 20,000 establishments serving a wide variety of food. The listing is by no means complete – but then again, neither is the AA's – although the directory is expanding all the time and if your favourite isn't listed you can always add it yourself, if you don't mind paying £99 for the privilege.

Curry Pages www.currypages.com

If you like curry, you'll love Curry Pages which contains a listing of thousands of Indian restaurants across the UK, including reviews by normal people who eat there regularly rather than overpaid food critics. Admittedly this can make some of the reviews a little biased but, by and large, it's a very reliable resource for spice fans. Also accessible via WAP. For more of the same try Curry House (www.curryhouse.co.uk).

Top Table www.toptable.co.uk

Over 600 restaurants around the country are bookable from Top Table. Most of the establishments listed are based in the capital, as you might expect, but there's a few spread across the country (and even a couple in Paris) if you look hard enough. Assuming you can find a restaurant near you, the booking system is excellent and anecdotal evidence suggests that you can often get into 'unbookable' venues extremely easily. For European restaurants, try Last Minute (www.lastminute.com).

■ The best of the rest

Book 2 Eat www.book2eat.com

More table-booking facilities from another slick site. As with Top Table, the majority of decent restaurants are in London but if you do live in the capital, or are planning a visit, this could well be the easiest way to find a place to eat.

Fatty Arbuckle's www.fatty-arbuckles.co.uk
Big food for big appetites.

Harry Ramsdens www.harryramsdens.co.uk
Everything you ever wanted or needed to know about the world's most famous fish and chips.

Pizza Express www.pizzaexpress.co.uk
Ultra-hip site which gives you the opportunity to join the Pizza Express club. If you're a regular visitor you'll definitely want to check this out.

Pizza Hut www.pizzahut.co.uk
Find your nearest restaurant, be tempted by the new toppings and even chat to Dave the Helpful Tomato. Ok then.

The Fashion Cafe www.fashion-cafe.com
Eat with Naomi, Claudia and Elle at one of their worldwide locations. Looks good but lacks personality. Funny that. For even more glitz and glamour, take a trip to Planet Hollywood (www.planethollywood.com).

Pubs and bars

If you prefer a liquid lunch, the web is full of sites that promise to help you find your nearest watering hole. For starters, check out some of our recommendations – where everybody knows your name.

■ *The best of the best*

Brewers and Licensed Retailers Association www.blra.co.uk

The official site of the BLRA features more information about pubs and brewing than you could ever possibly need. Pub locations, beer news and information, drink driving advice (don't) and even taxation are covered on this superb resource – and, in the unlikely event that you can't find what you're looking for, there are plenty of links to external sites and resources.

■ *The rest of the best*

The Good Pub Guide www.goodpubs.co.uk

The main purpose of this site is to persuade you to buy one
of the company's 'Good Guide' books but even if you don't
want to part with your money, there's plenty to see. The real
crowd-puller is the (almost) complete database of the best
British pubs, searchable by location, which is free to browse
once you've registered as a visitor.

Pub World www.pubworld.co.uk

Pub World really does feature a whole world of pubs,
including a huge searchable database of the UK's finest.
Simply type in the town, style of pub or even the name and
you'll be presented with a list of possible matches. The site
also boasts loads of other useful information for dedicated
pub goers.

Real Ale Guide www.real-ale-guide.co.uk

Find your nearest real ale pub with this simple but effective
site.

Takeaways

Don't get too excited – the possibility of ordering food over
the internet and having it delivered to your door is still a
dream for the future for most of the UK. Having said that, a
growing number of takeaway food outlets are taking
advantage of the web to allow you to find your nearest pizza
place or burger joint – and if you live in a major city, the
growing popularity of online ordering means you may
never have to leave the house again. Great.

■ The best of the best

Takeaways www.takeaways.co.uk

The UK's most comprehensive takeaway food directory allows you to search for your nearest junk food emporium by location or type of cuisine. Not every region is covered yet but if you're looking for food in an unfamiliar place, there really is no better resource than 'your gateway to local takeaway'. Look out for other handy features, including a newsletter, TV listings and even chopstick lessons – couch potato heaven.

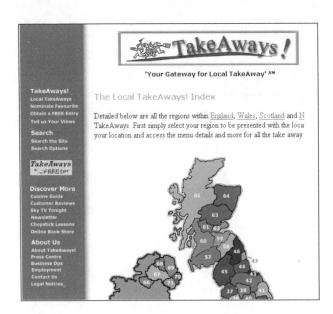

■ *The rest of the best*

Leaping Salmon www.leapingsalmon.co.uk

Proving that takeaways don't have to be about cardboard boxes and paper napkins, Leaping Salmon will deliver a gourmet meal anywhere in the UK within 24 hours. Unlike traditional takeaway food, this comes in uncooked form with detailed instructions on how to prepare everything, so you will have to spend a few minutes in the kitchen. The results, however, are well worth the wait and the extra effort. If you live in London and would prefer not to have to do any of the cooking, try Room Service (www.roomservice.co.uk).

Domino's Pizza www.dominos.co.uk

Domino's were the first company in the UK to allow you to order pizza from any of their nationwide outlets. Simply sign up to the service, locate your nearest Domino's, place your order and wait for delivery – couldn't be easier really.

McDonald's www.mcdonalds.co.uk

McDonald's have a predictably flashy web presence which provides information about the food, the restaurants and the popular television adverts. If you're planning a children's party or fancy a Happy Meal then you'll probably make good use of the restaurant finder – although, to be honest, it would probably be easier to list all of the places that *don't* have a McDonald's rather than those that do.

Burger King www.burgerking.co.uk

The home of the Whopper, and arch rival to McDonald's has obviously put a lot of effort (and money) into this extremely funky website which allows you to build your own burger and win big prizes. If you have a slow connection, watch out for slow loading and loads of pop-up windows.

■ *The best of the rest*

KFC www.kfc.co.uk

More store locations, job opportunities and corporate blurb plus plenty of smiling pictures of the Colonel.

Little Chef www.little-chef.co.uk

Location information, competitions and even 10 per cent off for site visitors. Small but perfectly formed.

Perfect Pizza www.perfectpizza.co.uk

Find your nearest restaurant, get a job or just find out more about the company.

Still looking?

Although we've tried to cover the most useful and interesting online food and drink resources we're not infallible (hard to believe but true!).

If you can't find the information you're looking for, why not visit us on the web? The Zingin Food and Drink Guide (www.zingin.com/guide/leisure/food) contains all of the sites listed here plus an up-to-date directory of the best new resources for drinkers and diners.

Don't panic if you're still having no luck, just surf over to our Search Guide (www.zingin.com/guide/search) where our team of human search experts will try their hardest to help you out – and it won't cost you a penny!

quick reference guide

General portals

Specialist portals

Recipe databases

Alternative recipes

Ingredients

Popular food brands

Dieting and weight loss

Nutrition and healthy eating

Wine portals and information

Vineyards and regions

Wine making and selling

Spirits

Cocktails

Beer guides and portals

Breweries

Cobra	www.cobrabeer.com	62
Fosters	www.fostersbeer.com	62
Grolsch	www.grolsch.com	62
Guinness	www.guiness.ie	62
Heineken	www.heineken.com	62
Kronenbourg	www.kronenbourg1664.co.uk	62
Labatts	www.labatt.com	63
Scrumpy Jack	www.scrumpyjack.com	63
Shepherd Neame	www.shepherd-neame.co.uk	63
Thwaites	www.thwaites.co.uk	63

Tea and coffee

Koffee Korner	www.koffeekorner.com	66
Smell the Coffee	www.smellthecoffee.com	64
Tea	www.tea.co.uk	65
Tea and Coffee	www.teaandcoffee.net	66
Tea Health	www.teahealth.co.uk	65
Tea Time	www.teatime.com	66
The Coffee Club	www.coffee.co.uk	66

Fizzy drinks

Coca Cola	www.cocacola.com	67
Dr Pepper	www.drpepper.com	69
Evian	www.evian.com	70
Irn Bru	www.irn-bru.co.uk	68
Lucozade	www.lucozade.co.uk	69
Pepsi	www.pepsi.co.uk	68
Perrier	www.perrier.com	70
Soda Fountain	www.sodafountain.com	66
Tango	www.tango.co.uk	68

Drink

Directories and department stores

Specialist suppliers

Restaurants

Pubs and bars

Takeaways

Zingin links

| Feedback (E-mail) | feedback@zingin.com |
| Feedback (Form) | www.zingin.com/feedback.html |

Home	www.zingin.com
Search Guide	www.zingin.com/guide/search
Suggest a Site	www.zingin.com/add.html
Food and Drink Guide	www.zingin.com/guide/leisure/food